James and Elizabeth,
a True Story of Brave Ohio Pioneers

James and Elizabeth, a True Story of Brave Ohio Pioneers

Nancy Lynn Marlowe Scranton
(June 29, 1946 – July 21, 2009)

This book is dedicated to my husband, James Scranton, the great-great-great-grandson of James and Elizabeth Whitaker, our beloved children, Paul, Abigail and Peter, and our grandchildren, Sean, Cieran, Bridget, Elizabeth, and Charlotte.

Illustrations by Pat Bristley

Compiled by Abigail Marlowe Scranton Woodman

Copyright © 2012, Nancy Scranton

All rights reserved. No part of this book may be reproduced, stored, or transmitted by any means—whether auditory, graphic, mechanical, or electronic—without written permission of both publisher and author, except in the case of brief excerpts used in critical articles and reviews. Unauthorized reproduction of any part of this work is illegal and is punishable by law.

ISBN 978-1-105-65887-7

Nancy Scranton with her husband and grandchildren, April 2009

This book was originally conceived by my mother, Nancy Scranton. Nancy always enjoyed hearing stories about my father's ancestors, the Whitakers. She wanted her grandchildren to be able to read about them, so she began researching to write a children's book. When she died, I finished the book with help from my husband, Britain.

Though Nancy was not an Ohio native, she grew to love the state, and cherished her family's connection to the history of Northwest Ohio.

~Abbey

Contents

Chapter 1	Peninsula dwellers	1
Chapter 2	Elizabeth comes to Ohio	7
Chapter 3	"This is my son. You must not kill him!"	11
Chapter 4	Fine china on the frontier	17
Chapter 5	As mean as dirt	21
Chapter 6	The foul aspersions of her slanderous tongue	25
Chapter 7	Great credit for your exertions	31
Chapter 8	That brave and stout-hearted woman	37
Chapter 9	A barrel of rotten pork	41
Appendix		45
Works Referenced		59

Wyandot pony race by the Sandusky River. Illustration by Pat Bristley.

Chapter 1
Peninsula dwellers

French explorers and Jesuit missionaries began to survey the area now known as Ohio in the 1580s. Upon arrival, they met two groups of American Indians living along the shores of Lake Erie. They named the tribe living north of Lake Erie, the Huron, and the tribe living in the Ohio area was named the Erie. For the next hundred years, these two tribes battled with the Iroquois from the New York area. The Iroquois had better weapons, including steel tomahawks, from trading with the Dutch settlers in New York. They pushed the Erie and Huron people westward, and by the mid-1650s, they had been forced out of the area they once called home. For nearly a century, very few people lived in the Ohio area.

By the 1750s, many American Indians had returned to Ohio, because the British colonists and new settlers were pushing the eastern American Indian tribes westward. The Erie and Huron tribes were also returning to the Ohio area. All of the tribes united under the name of Wendat (the white settlers called them Wyandot). One of their major villages was located at the current site of Fremont, Ohio. The American Indians did not want settlers in their area. They tolerated the French traders, as they only visited to trade fur, not to establish settlements. The French constructed a trading post in Lower Sandusky (now Fremont) in the 1750s, to trade with the Wyandots.

The American Indians even allied with the French during the French and Indian War (1754–1763), fighting against the British and colonists. In the aftermath of the conflict, the British assumed control of the Lower Sandusky area. However, the British also chose to respect American Indian lands, earning the Indians' support in the Revolutionary War (1775–1783).

The Wyandots were mostly made up of descendants of the Iroquois. Though they are rarely referred to as Iroquois, they did speak the Iroquois language and shared many of the Iroquois traditions. Originally, they lived north of the Iroquois, in the Lake Simcoe region of Ontario. The French first called them Huron, which means "rough" or "boar." They thought the Indians, with their Mohawks, looked like wild boars. However, the Hurons referred to themselves as Wendat, or Guyandot, meaning "peninsula dwellers" or "islanders." The Huron name is more widely used for tribes that lived in Canada; the Wyandot was used for the descendants of the tribe that moved to what is now the United States.

Huron-Wendat Hunter Calling a Moose, by Cornelius Krieghoff (1815-1872), about 1868.

    The Wyandots usually lived on high ground near a river. They constructed a wall, or palisade, to protect the villages from raids. During most of the year, they lived in longhouses made with pole frames and covered by elm or cedar bark. The longhouses were about ninety to one hundred feet long and fifteen to twenty feet wide. They had a rectangular base, a domed roof, and no windows. People slept along the walls and the center area was used for cooking and ceremonies.

    Wyandots had a matriarchal family structure. After marriage, the couple would live with the wife's family together in one longhouse. Longhouses often had several sisters, their husbands and children, and the parents, all living together.

A Wendat longhouse, photographed in Midland, Ontario, Canada. The Wyandot of Ohio lived together in similar structures. Photograph by Douglas M. Paine, Copyright © 2009. Used with permission.

One ceremony that was important to them was the Dance of Fire. Dancers carried hot coals or heated stones in their mouths and thrust their arms in boiling water. It was meant to invoke a spirit, or Oki, to heal the sick. Also, every decade or so, the tribe held a Feast of the Dead to honor dead relatives. The remains of their relatives were brought back from the cemetery, and over a feast, villagers shared remembrances of the dead.

Shamans were men who led the religious ceremonies, and told stories about the history of the tribe. The Wyandots believed that the earth was created by Sky Woman, or Aataentsic. She fell to the world that was covered by oceans and landed on the back of a giant turtle. She had twin sons: Iouskeha (the good twin) and Tawiscaron (the bad twin). All the children were taught the tribe's history. Storytelling was common, especially during bad weather.

The women made their clothing from buckskin and beaver pelts, which were often fringed and painted with designs. Men wore moccasins and breechcloths in the warm months. Women wore knee-length buckskin skirts. When it was cold, the men wore long-sleeved shirts and leggings and had beaver cloaks. Women had fur robes as well. They wore their hair long and usually braided. Men often wore their hair long, or cut it in the Mohawk style. Some dyed their hair. Most men also had a fire pouch to carry their tobacco and pipes. Both men and women wore necklaces and bracelets made from wampum, beads made from seashells. Women also wore earrings and belts of wampum or bone. Sometimes they painted their faces with vegetable or mineral dyes.

A young native wearing Huron-Wendat traditional dress and paint takes part in the dance contest of the Wendake Pow-Wow, July 31, 2010. Copyright © 2010 Francis Vachon - info@francisvachon.com. Used with permission.

The women cooked, worked in the fields, and gathered wild berries, cherries, and grapes as well as acorns and walnuts. They grew many crops, including corn, beans, squash, and tobacco for smoking. The Wyandots made maple syrup from a grove located in the Clyde, Ohio area. The women also hauled wood and stripped basswood bark to make it into rope.

The men hunted deer, wildcat, woodchuck, raccoon, beaver, birds, and bear. Sometimes they chased deer into rivers or fenced areas and then killed them with bows and arrows. Birds were either shot with bows or caught in nets. Beavers and bears were caught in traps. The bears were often fed and fattened for a year or two before being eaten. The Black Swamp area (north and west of present-day Fremont, Ohio) was one of their favorite hunting grounds. They also fished using birch bark canoes. They caught walleye, catfish, pike, and other fish. To catch them, they used bone hooks, harpoons, traps, spears, or large nets woven from nettles. Sometimes the men would spend a month or more on the islands, fishing.

If the soil in one area became infertile or game or wood became scarce, the Wyandots moved their villages. This happened about every ten to twenty years.

Wyandot babies were carried in wooden cradleboards with moss or cattail cushions. They were breastfed for the first two to three years. The mothers would chew the food first and then give bits of it to the babies once they were old enough to eat solid food. The babies would sleep naked between the mother and father.

Wyandot adults were very affectionate with their children. The children were rarely disciplined and had a lot of freedom. However, they all were taught to contribute to the good of the community. They were expected to be tough, so they wore little clothing, even in winter.

Children of all ages were given responsibilities. Young boys and girls had to help weed the fields and chase birds away. Boys had to learn to use bows and arrows and spears. Between chores, they competed in games to strengthen their hunting skills. One game was called "snow snake." They slid a curved stick across snow and the stick that went the farthest won. They also enjoyed lacrosse. There was pony racing too. They learned to make tools and build longhouses.

Girls were sent to collect water and gather firewood. They were also taught to cook and care for their younger siblings and to store food, sew, make pottery, and weave nets and baskets.

The city of Fremont is located where two Indian trails crossed. The Warrior's Path stretched from what is now Kentucky to Lake Erie; the Lake Trail, extended from Cleveland to Detroit. The Sandusky River Valley was part of territory claimed by both France and England. It was also an area that had Indian trade rivalries. The British established headquarters in the Fremont area to supply weapons to their Indian allies during the Revolutionary War. The Indians would go on raids in the East, sometimes as far away as New York and Kentucky.

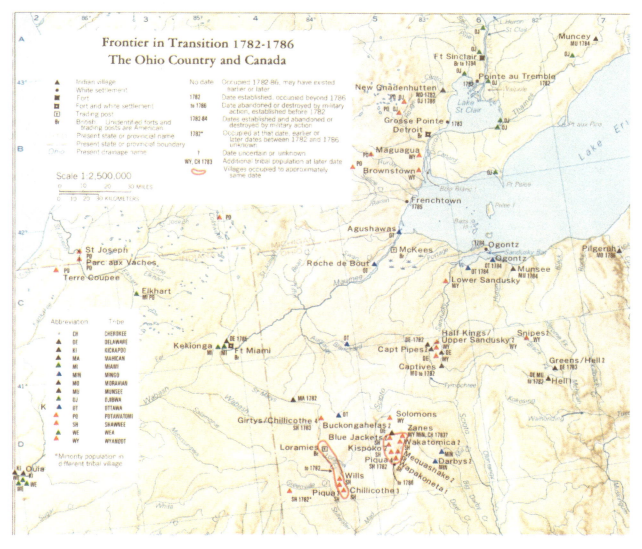

Tanner, Helen Hornbeck. *Atlas of Great Lakes Indian History*. Norman: Published for the Newberry Library by the University of Oklahoma Press, 1987. Detail from page 85.

Wyandot warriors sneak up on Elizabeth and others while the settlers boil maple syrup in the woods. Illustration by Pat Bristley.

Chapter 2

Elizabeth comes to Ohio

Elizabeth Foulks was born on December 25, 1765, in Leesburg, Virginia to William and Nancy Foulks. William Foulks was a farmer and soldier in the Pennsylvania militia. Nancy preferred to be called by the name Anne. In 1768, at Fort Stanwix in New York, representatives of the Six Nations, or Iroquois, signed the Treaty of Fort Stanwix with the British. The treaty was signed to set the boundary line between American Indian lands and colonial settlements. The British government wanted to end frontier violence, and the American Indians wanted a permanent line to hold back British colonists. The new boundary ran near Fort Pitt and followed the Ohio River to the Tennessee River. Instead of promoting peace, it led to more violence.

Colonial settlers continued to battle with the American Indians, who had treaty rights to hunt in the Ohio Valley. Lord Dunmore, royal governor of Virginia, decided to declare a state of war in early 1774. The war ended quickly when Virginia claimed victory in the Battle of Point Pleasant on October 10, 1774. American Indians lost the right to hunt in the area, and the Shawnee and Mingo tribes finally agreed to recognize the Ohio River as the boundary between Indian and colonial lands.

Several other tribes, however, continued to refuse to recognize the treaty. Moreover, some settlers continued to invade the land held by the Indians. As a result, murders and kidnappings became prevalent along the border of the Ohio River. Both the settlers and American Indians did their share of killing.

The Foulks family moved to this embattled border region in 1774. At the time, it was claimed by both Virginia and Pennsylvania; presently it is known as Beaver Creek, Pennsylvania. William had wanted to build houses in Leesburg, but lost his money. He had hoped that a farm on the western frontier would provide a better life. However, he died while working the land. He left seven children: John, born in 1761; Catherine, born in 1762; Elizabeth, 1765; Henry born in 1767; William II, 1768; George, 1769; and Jacob, 1771. Their mother, Anne, soon married William Tucker, another farmer. Anne and her children moved in with the Tucker family, which included William, Lewis, and Polly Tucker.

Elizabeth's new home was close to hundreds of maple trees. Maple trees have sap that can be easily processed to make sugar. And, they could be tapped to make sweet maple syrup that children loved. Usually spouts were carved from pine, maple, or sumac trees. Troughs were set up near the base of the trees to catch the sap. They would boil the sap over an open fire in large kettles, and then it was put into smaller kettles to make sugar. The children of local families would often work together to collect and process the sap. Older boys and young men would carry guns to protect the children.

On March 20, 1776, when Elizabeth was eleven, she, two of her siblings, her three step-siblings, and other children from the Turner, Walker, McKeever, and Casselman families were collecting sap from these trees. At least fifteen young people worked in the grove over the course of eight days, making sugar. The grove was near Raccoon Creek. A group of Wyandots happened upon the sugar camp. However, the older boys were armed and firing at practice targets on the trees, so the Wyandots waited until nighttime. After the children had settled for the night, the Wyandots attacked!

John Foulks, Elizabeth's older brother, ran from the Indians and tripped over his dog, allowing the warriors to catch up to him. John and the other older children were killed and scalped (British commanders offered a bounty for settlers' scalps to encourage hostility between the American settlers and Indians.). This group of Wyandots was from the village of the Wyandot Chief known to the British as Half King, or as Dunquat by other Wyandots.

The Wyandots killed at least four of the group and kept the youngest children, including Elizabeth and her brother George, as captives. The other captives included Polly and Lewis Tucker, Elizabeth and John Turner, and Margaret and Mary Casselman. Each captive received moccasins to wear on the long trip back to the Wyandot camp in Northwest Ohio. The girls' gowns were slit to help them walk more easily. To cross the Ohio River, the Wyandots made their prisoners cling to logs and pushed them across the river.

George had been wounded in the attack by a tomahawk to his head. This injury made the already rough trip particularly difficult for him. Only the girls were allowed to ride the horses, though Elizabeth would occasionally dismount her horse to allow George a short ride. When the Wyandots noticed, they would pull George from the horse and make him continue on foot. Three days into the trip, the Wyandots finally treated George's wound with elm bark and bear's oil.

When they reached the Tuscarawas River in what is now Eastern Ohio (west of Pittsburgh, PA), the water level was high. The Indians had no canoe. As with the Ohio River crossing, they cut down trees and tied the children to them. The Indians swam and pushed the trees across the river.

When the children arrived at the Wyandot camp in Northwest Ohio, they were given a feast of venison, wild turkey, and hominy. The children were all adopted into the tribe. Adoption of white children was a common American Indian ritual to replace children lost in conflict with colonists. This ritual involved wading naked into the Sandusky River and being washed with pebbles by the female members of their new families. The chief, Half King, adopted Elizabeth. He appreciated her loyalty to her brother and admired her fearlessness.

The children adapted to life in the Wyandot camp. As with children born into the tribe, the boys learned hunting and tracking skills, and the girls learned how to care for the homes and cook. They learned the culture, language, habits, and lands of the Wyandots in Ohio. When smallpox threatened, the Indians used a natural method to guard the family—they caught skunks and allowed them to spray their odor in the wigwam.

The children also had to help in the fields. One day when Elizabeth and George were hoeing corn in a field, they discovered a swarm of bees. The Indians had never seen bees before. The children had, though; the superstitious Indians took this as a sign that the bees belonged to white people, and that white settlers were coming.

Later, Polly Tucker married a French trader named Wine. She returned to Pennsylvania after 1795. Lewis Tucker escaped. Elizabeth Turner married Alexander McCormick. They moved to Ontario in 1796; Alexander would fight for the British in the War of 1812. George Foulks married a Wyandot woman and had two children with her but left for home around 1790. He later joined the military and became a spy for the Americans under Captain Samuel Brady. Margaret and Mary Casselman's father paid George to go steal them back from the Wyandots. George later married Catherine Ullery in 1796 and had eleven more children with her. Elizabeth Foulks married fellow Wyandot captive James Whitaker.

James running the Gauntlet. Illustration by Pat Bristley.

Chapter 3

"This is my son. You must not kill him!"

James Whitaker was born in London, England in 1756. In 1767, at the age of twelve, he sailed to New York on his uncle's sailing schooner. James wandered away from the ship, and his uncle, Captain John Whitaker, was unable to find him. Eventually John Whitaker sailed back to England. A descendant of the Whitaker family, Mrs. Effie Whitaker Teemer, said she believed Captain John had been killed by pirates.

James Whitaker became a member of the garrison at Fort Pitt, in western Pennsylvania, under the command of Colonel Brodhead. Fort Pitt is now known as Pittsburgh, Pennsylvania. In 1774, when James was eighteen, he accompanied his older brother, Quill, and another soldier on a hunting trip. They were at Fish Creek searching for game to hunt. A group of Wyandot Indians attacked and killed the soldier. However, Quill survived by running away. James tried to flee too, but was hit in the arm by a rifle ball, captured, and taken to a village called Captain Snips in present-day Richland County, Ohio.

Over two thousand captives were brought to, or through, Lower Sandusky, Ohio, in the 1700s and early 1800s. It was a frequent stopping point for tribes on their way to Detroit. The British encouraged raids on Kentucky and Ohio settlers. In addition to buying scalps, the British offered one hundred dollars in gold for each captive. They would then demand ransom from the colonials' families. If they stayed with the tribes, the women, children, or black captives usually became slaves. James was eighteen when captured, so like all males of his age, he was forced to run the gauntlet in order to live, in spite of his wounded arm.

The gauntlet was a path, twenty to forty yards long, through which the captives would have to run. Their goal was a large stake, usually painted, in the ground. All the tribe members, including the children, would form rows down the path. The captives were stripped naked and disorientated through blows to their heads. Then they had to run. The spectators would throw rocks or dirt at the runners. They would also spit at them or try to trip them. Sometimes they would use sticks to beat on them. If the man fell, he would be beaten until he died, passed out, or struggled to his feet. Sometimes the captives were made to run the gauntlet more than once. Refusing to run or hesitating usually led to execution. Bravery, however, was highly valued. The Wyandot gauntlet in present-day Fremont, Ohio, extended from what is now State Street, on the west side of the Sandusky River, north to the railroad bridge—the same route along which Wyandot boys raced ponies.

James was nearing the end of the gauntlet when an elderly squaw grabbed his wounded arm. James kicked her, and the squaw and several other Wyandots fell. He continued to the stake post. Many were upset that James ran the gauntlet too quickly and insisted he run it again. However, his bravery impressed another elderly squaw, who threw a blanket around him and said, "This is my son. He is one of us. You must not kill him." She adopted him and treated him with kindness and affection.

James Whitaker was one captive who survived the gauntlet and earned the respect of his captors. He later became a chief in the Wyandot tribe. His bravery, and later, his support of their way of life, made him a valued member of the tribe.

On January 5, 1778, the signature of James Whitaker appears on a proclamation issued by British lieutenant governor Henry Hamilton. Henry Hamilton was a notorious scalp hunter; however, Hamilton's letter concerned the humane and kind treatment several American captives had received from both American Indian and white captors. The proclamation was signed by James Whitaker and other captives.

Excerpt of proclamation:

> We who have undersigned our names, do voluntarily declare that we have been conducted from the several places mentioned opposite our names to Detroit by Indians accompanied with white people; that we have neither been cruelly treated nor in any way ill used by them; and further that on our arrival we have been treated with the greatest humanity and our wants supplied in the best manner possible.

James Whitaker, from Fort Pitt, taken at Fish Creek

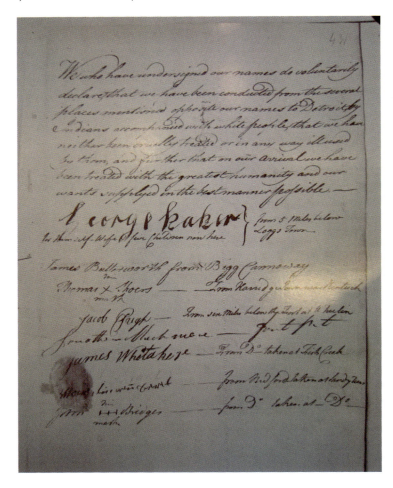

First record of James' capture.

James Whitaker met Elizabeth Foulks several years later. In written correspondence, Thomas Williams of Detroit said James wanted to marry Elizabeth because "she was growing up wild and he intended to civilize her." James remembered the settlers' customs, as he was older when he was captured.

James paid for her freedom from the tribe with four gallons of rum, according to a letter written by William Arundel, a British trader, to Thomas Williams, another trader. In the letter dated August 31, 1782, Arundel asks for four gallons of rum: "Whitaker would be obliged if you would please send him the same quantity and charge to his account—directing the keg for him. He has married a white prisoner girl lately. With the above he intends to get her entirely clear of the Indians. Mr. Robins married them."

William Arundel and Obidiah Robbins were both British, two of the first traders in the area. They had a trading post at the foot of the lower rapids of the Sandusky River. James and Elizabeth probably had two marriage ceremonies, one in Lower Sandusky in a Wyandot ceremony and aided by Obidiah Robbins and another later, in Detroit, presided over by a minister. The Wyandots gifted them with 1280 acres of fertile land on the west side of the river valley. It is north of what is now Fremont, Ohio. After their marriage in 1782, they settled on that land in a log cabin.

Marriage of James and Elizabeth in Lower Sandusky. Illustration by Pat Bristley.

White people who settled these lands were in direct violation of the Treaty of Greeneville. However, James was not a United States citizen; both he and Elizabeth were captured prior to the colonies winning independence. He was captured in 1774 and Elizabeth was captured in 1776. Some might call them more British than American.

However, the Treaty of Paris in 1782 ended the Revolutionary War. Much of the land Great Britain had won in the French and Indian War was ceded to the United States. In 1787, the United States Congress passed the Northwest Ordinance, which opened the western territory to settlement. This included the area where the Whitakers lived.

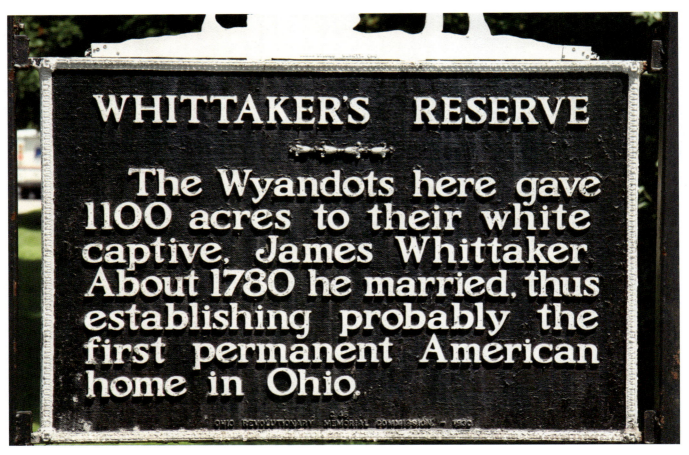

Historical marker for Whitaker Reserve. Photograph © 2010 Dale K. Benington. Used with permission.

James built Elizabeth a two-story frame house. Illustration by Pat Bristley.

Chapter 4
Fine china on the frontier

James and Elizabeth initially lived in a log cabin that James built. Most white traders and Wyandots lived in log cabins, but James longed to live with his wife in a proper house, the way he had grown up. A few years later, James traded furs and American Indian supplies for lumber from Canada. He had it rafted up the Sandusky River and built a two-story house—the first frame house built in Ohio. He also built a store, a warehouse, and docks on the river. With this house, James and Elizabeth became the first permanent continuous white settlers within the borders of Ohio.

James excelled at trading and soon grew wealthy. In a letter written by James Mackintosh, he tells Solomon Sibley, a Whitaker family attorney, that James had amassed about $12,000 by the fall of 1798. Anyone with assets of $5,000 or more was considered wealthy. Though James remained loyal to the American Indians and the British suppliers, he also earned the trust of settlers. He had two trading posts near the largest Wyandot villages: Lower Sandusky and Tymochtee, which is in present-day Wyandot County, Ohio. Later, he opened a post in Upper Sandusky.

He signed a trading agreement in 1794 with several other traders in the area, including Isaac Williams, Sr., Isaac Williams, Jr., Francois DuChouquet, Joseph Borrel, and Israel Ruland.

James and Elizabeth's first child, Nancy, was born in 1783. Nancy is believed to be the first child of two white parents born in Ohio. Elizabeth took her first trip home to Beaver Creek when Nancy was nine months old. She held the baby on horseback, escorted by two Wyandot squaws. James and Elizabeth also had Isaac, James Junior, Mary (born 1791), Elizabeth, Charlotte, Rachel (born 1801), and George (born 1803).

In addition to the frame house, they lived a privileged life, more characteristic of New York sophisticates than settlers on the frontier. They drank imported tea out of china teacups from Europe. They braved the elements in fur hats from London.

The letter from James below mentions wanting a hat for his wife:

James Whitaker to Thos Williams, Detroit,
Sandusky May, 1783

Sir: I shall be glad you will send 1 Kegg of Rum 4 gallons and 1 of 2 gallons, 1 White Beaver Hatt for my Wife and 2 Black Beaver Hatts, 1 lb Bohea Tea the tea you sent to Mr. Dawson to the Shawney town. Rec. 1/4 only the tea, please charge Mr. Dawson & C.

I am your humble svt.
J. Whitaker

James visited Montreal, Canada once or twice a year to trade furs. He took Nancy, his eldest, on one trip, and they visited with a British family named Wilson. Nancy went with one of their daughters to Glasgow, Scotland to be educated; she would spend three years at school there. James had received an education and wrote well; however, Elizabeth could only dictate letters and sign her name. She had been captured at such a young age that she had received no formal education. Though it cost the Whitaker family eight hundred dollars a year in tuition, both James and Elizabeth wanted Nancy, and all their children, to receive an education. Nancy returned home and educated her siblings.

Shortly after her return home, Nancy received a visitor: William Wilson, a British officer and son of the Montreal family who hosted her. After a whirlwind courtship, they married at the Whitaker home in 1799. William and Nancy lived with the Whitakers and entertained many British visitors over the years. Nancy had two girls and a boy and then passed away in 1804. William Wilson was called to England in 1810 to assume his position as Captain. Elizabeth kept William and Nancy's three children with her until the end of the War of 1812.

Battle of Fallen Timbers. Illustration by Pat Bristley.

Chapter 5

As mean as dirt

James and Elizabeth were often kind to American Indian captives, as they could relate to them. However, they had to walk a fine line between helping them and angering their Indian friends.

On March 20, 1790, Peggy Fleming, from Pittsburgh, Pennsylvania, and four others were attacked by Cherokee Indians on the Ohio River. Peggy's sister and a man were killed immediately. Peggy and two men were taken captive and held at a Cherokee camp in Lower Sandusky. Word quickly spread among area traders that the Cherokees had painted a captive black. James knew what this meant—that she would be tied to a wooden stake and burned alive. The traders visited the Cherokee camp in what is now known as Spiegel Grove. James and Peggy recognized each other at once. Her family owned a tavern in Pittsburgh that James enjoyed visiting when in the area for trading. Peggy begged for his help, and James agreed. He tried to convince the Cherokees to release her, but they refused.

The remains of Peggy Fleming's tree stayed in its original location until it began to rot.

By this time, James had earned a chief's title in the Wyandot tribe. He went to the principal chief, Chief Tarhe, for help. James claimed Peggy was his sister. Tarhe went to the Cherokee camp and asked them to release her as a favor; he told them that Peggy was the sister of a friend. When they refused, he offered money for her. They accused him of colluding with white people: "You are as mean as dirt," they told him.

The Cherokees' chiding compelled Tarhe to consider force, but he was reluctant to trigger war between the Wyandots and Cherokees. James and some fellow traders collected silver brooches to purchase her. Tarhe and eight or ten of his warriors returned to the Cherokee camp. When they arrived, the Cherokees were asleep. Peggy was tied to a tree, naked and painted black. Tarhe cut Peggy's ropes and took her into his custody, leaving the silver. The Wyandots escorted Peggy to James Whitaker's home. A few days later, James sent her back to Pittsburgh, disguised as a Wyandot and in the company of two Wyandot warriors. The Cherokees were outraged about Peggy's rescue. They entered the trading post in war paint and threatened vengeance. The traders laid in wait, weapons at the ready, but the Cherokee war party soon left the area. James was never in danger, as he was considered a Wyandot.

Another captive James Whitaker tried to help was Daniel Convers. He was captured on April 29, 1791 by a group of nine American Indians. He was taken near Fort Frye, now present-day Beverly, Ohio in Washington County. They arrived in Lower Sandusky in early May on their way to Detroit. James gave the captors a loaf of maple sugar to put them in a good mood so they would not harm Daniel. Daniel was also given a piece. Whitaker tried not to communicate with Daniel, so the Indians would not be angry. Daniel was able to return to his family and told of Whitaker's kindness.

Elizabeth also helped provide comfort to captives like Major Nathan Goodale from Marietta, Ohio, a veteran of the Revolutionary War. Goodale was captured on March 1, 1793, by eight Wyandots from his land near Belpre, Ohio. When he arrived in Lower Sandusky, he was very ill. The Indians did not think he could survive the trip to Detroit, so they left him at the Whitaker home with James and Elizabeth. Elizabeth made him comfortable and provided care until he died. She believed he died of a disease like pleurisy. He was buried in the Whitaker graveyard.

In addition to helping captives, they continued to help their adopted family as well. James Whitaker often participated in their war parties.

Arthur St. Clair, governor of the Northwest Territory, was told in 1791 to take troops through Ohio and build forts along the way. By November 4, 1791, they were in present-day Mercer County, Ohio, where they were ambushed by Indians led by Little Turtle of the Miamis and Blue Jacket of the Shawnees. In what is often called the "bloodiest battle of pioneer American history," St. Clair lost almost seven hundred men, while only forty Indians died. The fight—called both the Battle of Wabash and St. Clair's Defeat—only lasted three hours. The survivors fled south; the Indians did not pursue them. James Whitaker fought alongside the Indians as a Wyandot chief during this battle.

St. Clair resigned, and President George Washington placed his hopes for resolution on Anthony Wayne, whom he appointed commander of the United States Army of the Northwest in 1792. Wayne and his men were charged with defending settlers in the Northwest Territory from Indian attacks. He arrived in the area in May 1793 with troop reinforcements.

Wayne drilled his troops regularly. He ordered the construction of two new forts as well. Fort Greene Ville was built six miles north of Fort Jefferson. On the site of St. Clair's defeat, Wayne optimistically named the new fort "Recovery."

A group of five hundred warriors from the Shawnee, Miami, Ottawa, Delaware, and Ojibwa tribes, led by Little Turtle of the Miami tribe, attacked a supply train between Fort Recovery and Fort Greene Ville on June 30, 1794. Many of the white Americans were killed or captured. Wayne moved into northwestern Ohio later that summer, ordering construction of Fort Defiance. Wayne also had his men destroy Indian villages and crops in the area. Little Turtle and Tarhe wanted to settle their differences, but the Shawnee leader, Blue Jacket, refused.

Again, James Whitaker chose to fight alongside the Indians in what would be known as the Battle of Fallen Timbers. This formerly densely wooded area was known as Fallen Timbers after a tornado knocked down many trees. It is now present-day Maumee, Ohio. The Indians expected the army on August 19th, and fasted before battle to prepare. In addition to cultural and spiritual reasons, it was practical to avoid having food in their stomachs—if wounded, the chance of infection decreased significantly on an empty stomach. However, the troops did not arrive until August 20th, and the Indians were weak with hunger.

The Indians used the fallen trees for cover, but the troops overwhelmed them. Wayne lost thirty-three men and counted approximately one hundred wounded. Indian casualties were double. Tarhe was wounded, but survived. Blue Jacket and the other Indians retreated and asked for help from the British at Fort Miami. The British refused to help. The Indians gave up.

In a twist of fate, it is possible that James' brother-in-law, George Foulks, fought on the side of the Americans. A few years prior, in 1791, he had left the Wyandot tribe and returned to Pennsylvania. After leaving the Wyandot tribe, George worked as a scout for the Americans for several years and used his knowledge of American Indian life to spy on them.

Wayne and the Indians negotiated a treaty and signed it on August 3, 1795. The Treaty of Greeneville included over one thousand Indians from several tribes, including the Wyandot, Shawnee, Miami, Ottawa, and Delaware. Tarhe's name was the first signed under General Wayne. They all agreed to give up their land in the Ohio Valley and move to the northwest part of what is now Ohio. The northwest part of Ohio was known as the Black Swamp. Few whites wanted to settle there, as it was too wet to farm or settle. Northwestern Ohio became part of the Wayne Indian Reservation. What is now Sandusky County was part of Indian land. The American Indians were also granted the right to hunt on lands not settled. Tecumseh refused to attend the signing of the treaty. He also did not move onto the land the treaty assigned him. He believed the land could not belong to anyone. In a letter sent in 1810 to William Henry Harrison, who was at the time the territorial governor of Indian Territory, Tecumseh wrote "Sell a country! Why not sell the air, the clouds, and the great sea, as well as the earth? Did not the Great Spirit make them all for the use of his children?"

After the Treaty of Greeneville, pioneers moved into the Lower Sandusky area. The United States built a fortified trading post there. However, the British kept supplying some Indians with rifles. The settlers still felt unsafe and asked the US Government for help. The army built Fort Stephenson to help protect the residents of Lower Sandusky.

Trading post on the Whitaker Reserve. Illustration by Pat Bristley.

Chapter 6
The foul aspersions of her slanderous tongue

Indiana Territory was formed on July 4, 1800. It included all of present-day Indiana, Illinois, and Wisconsin and parts of Minnesota, Michigan, and Ohio. The Northwest Territory was essentially present-day Ohio, and the part that was in Indiana Territory became part of Ohio when it was admitted as a state on March 1, 1803.

During this time, James expanded his trading business. Canadians Richard and Hugh Pattinson convinced James to enter into a partnership with them. Together, they founded a new trading company, Whitaker and Pattinson. Hugh Pattinson assumed control of Whitaker's trading post at Upper Sandusky. However, Hugh's appropriation of company funds caused the partnership to collapse. Correspondence from the time includes Hugh making excuses to James and James growing skeptical of Hugh's character.

James asked for a statement of affairs, and Hugh replied that it could not be prepared until another matter with Richard was settled. In the letter written by Hugh to James dated September 24, 1802, Hugh tells him to wait and goes on to say, "You express taking disagreeable Measures if you think yourself wrong'd, You are perfectly at liberty so to do." Hugh also did not want James to access the company's accounting. From a letter dated September 27, 1802, from Hugh to James: "Should you want any extracts from the books of Whitaker & Pattinson or Mackintosh Whitaker & Pattinson they are always ready for you (myself present) but as to the giving of any out of my hands is a thing which I absolutely refuse to do."

On December 17, 1804, James traveled to Upper Sandusky to speak with Hugh Pattinson about the business. Upon his arrival, Hugh offered James a glass of wine. Soon after drinking it, James died. It is believed James was poisoned by Hugh.

His tombstone was brought from the Whitaker farm and placed in Birchard Public Library in Fremont, Ohio.

His tombstone reads:

IN MEMORY OF
JAMES WHITEACRE
WHO DIED
DEC. 17, 1804
In the 48th year of his age.

Hugh Pattinson never faced formal charges of murder, but evidence surfaced that he had forged papers and taken funds from the store. He had diverted two thousand pounds sterling to his personal account in Montreal. Margaretta Township in Erie County, Ohio was originally named for Pattinson. Its residents changed its name when they discovered his horrible reputation.

James had left Elizabeth a two thousand-pound credit at a Canadian trading house; and after James' death, she assumed control of the trading business. Elizabeth had to manage the business, maintain the home, and care for her family. Elizabeth had children ranging from Nancy, twenty-one, to an infant not quite a year old. Her oldest sons, Issac and James, helped as much as possible.

Elizabeth was a very successful trader, and the trading post continued to prosper. She entertained many visitors, including British officers, Indians of various tribes, traders, and travelers. Her influence among the Wyandots increased as well. She served as both a translator and advisor for them. She also forged friendships with both British and Americans. William Wilson, Nancy's husband and a British captain, remained in the area. The U.S. Army General Benjamin Harrison visited Elizabeth frequently, including a six-week stay when she nursed him back to health. She even welcomed a visit from Tecumseh, the Shawnee chief.

Reverend Badger was another recurring visitor. A Revolutionary solider who fought at Bunker Hill, Badger became a missionary to the Indians. After James' death, he continued to visit Elizabeth and perform tasks around the homestead. He hoed corn, helped dig a well, and wrote letters for her.

Hugh Pattinson continued to cause problems for Elizabeth; he owed her money and refused to split up surplus goods and livestock once shared. Elizabeth sent a note to Hugh asking to meet her to divide the cattle. In a response from Pattinson to Elizabeth dated August 17, 1805, Hugh says, "I cannot make up my mind to See You upon any friendly terms whatever this cannot Surprise You after the scurrilous abuse and bitter epithets you have maliciously and unjustly thrown out against me without any provocation whatever."

She followed up with a civil suit after some of her livestock disappeared. She believed Hugh, or someone working for him, stole her animals and destroyed some property.

Here is a portion of a letter written on her behalf to her lawyer Sibley on August 25, 1807, about continued problems with Hugh Pattinson: "the day before Christmas Mr. Pattirsons people Mr. John Wilson, Old Isaac Williams and Shevalliere, a french come and shot among Mrs. Whitakers cows and steers and wounded one steer which they killed the thirteenth day after the year 1805...and again men in Pattinson imploy came on the 25 December at night after all the family were in bed, attempted to brake her doors and besiege the house."

Hugh also accused Elizabeth and Reverend Badger of immoral behavior. A letter from Elizabeth follows, written to her attorney, Solomon Sibley.

"To: Mr. Solomon Sibley, Esq.
Sandusky Sept 4, 1807

Sir:

Hugh Pattinson has undertaken in various instances, to scandalize my character-- has gone into such lengths in libels against me, that I think it a duty I owe to my family and myself to call on him for a settlement of the business in a legal way. If he comes into Detroit I wish you to commence a suit against him on my behalf for $10,000 dollars damages.

Hugh Pattinson has in a complaint against Joseph Badger to Govenor Hull, stated "That the said Joseph Badger hath for a long time part and still doth live in a state of fornication and adultery at Sandusky afforesaid, and the same evil practices hath been guilty of at diverse other places within this Territory with Elizabeth Whitaker, wife of James Whitaker late of Sandusky, deceased, and with her doth cohabit as man and wife, unbecoming his character and dignity, and against the moral precepts of the religious office of his priesthood and to the evil example of all those which whom he is sent to preside and imulate the principals of religion and virtue." Again he writes in his reply to Mr. Badgers letter to His Excellency; directed to Gerry McDougall, Esq. "You who are acquainted from experience with the intreagues and jealouses of Mrs. Whitaker to engage the whole trade of their country to herself; and having personally suffered under the foul aspersions of her slanderous tongue, ought not to be surprised at the length she goes now with me" Again, "If I have four or eight barrels of liquor in my store, it is no more than his friend Mrs. Whitaker has".

The above are statements calculated to destroy my character and injure my fatherless children.

I am respectfully your obedient servant
Elizabeth X Whitaker

Witnesses: Sam S. Waterman

P.S. I enclose your a Detroit ten dollar note, and also a letter to Wm A. Macintosh

When Pattinson found out about the $10,000 suit, he signed a retraction before witnesses stating, "I was induced to implicate the character of the said Elizabeth only from the advice of my friends, and with a view of defending myself against allegations made by the said Joseph Badger against me." He might have also settled with some cash. Pattinson was no longer a problem for Elizabeth.

Through all this, Elizabeth carried on. Nancy, her eldest, had died soon after James in 1804. Elizabeth cared for Nancy's children. She hired a teacher in 1808 to help educate her children and grandchildren while she traveled for business and translated for the Indians and whites.

> Sandusky 14th April 1803
>
> Mrs E. Whitaker
>
> Madam
>
> having drawn in some of the Outstanding Credits belonging to the late Partnership of Whitaker & Pattinson. I would be glad to know in what manner they are to be disposed of — whether they are to be divided or appropriated to the payment of balance of the Mens wages still remaining unpaid. Your answer this evening will much oblige
>
> Madam
> Your Obt Servt
> H. Pattinson

Correspondence from Hugh Pattinson to Elizabeth Whitaker, April 14, 1803.

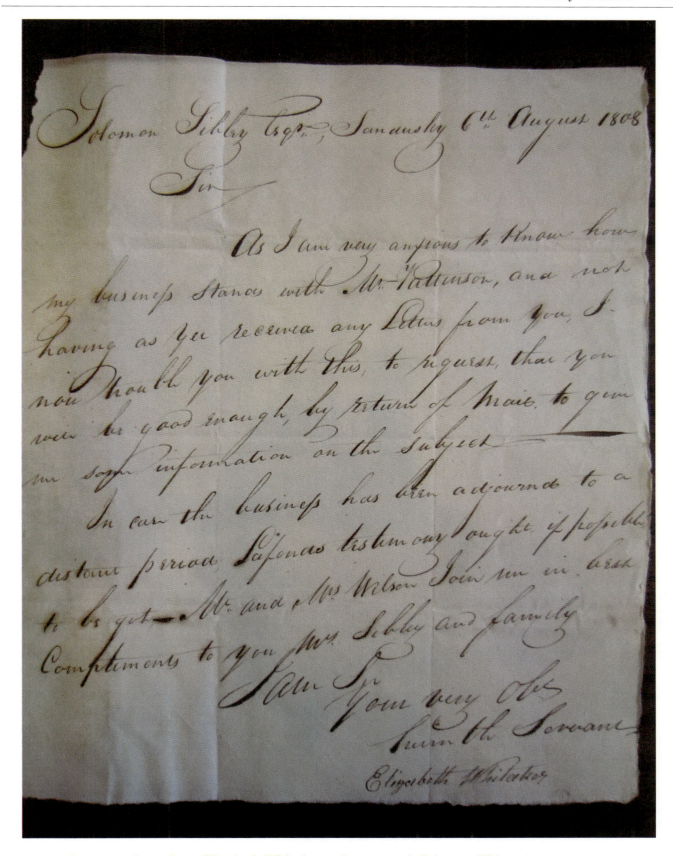

Correspondence from Elizabeth Whitaker to her counsel, Solomon Sibley, August 6, 1808.

Old Betsy, the cannon that saved Fort Stephenson, is located in front of the Birchard Public Library. The library was built on the fort's original site, in today's Fremont, OH.
Photograph © 2010 Dale K. Benington. Used with permission.

Chapter 7

Great credit for your exertions

Elizabeth remained friends with Reverend Badger and even helped him grow his ministry. Together, they worked to convince Tarhe, chief of the Wyandot tribe, to keep the Wyandots neutral during the War of 1812. Though she remained a friend of and ally to the Indians, Elizabeth was always loyal to the United States, particularly the Army.

Elizabeth learned a lot about the war from speaking with both the Wyandots and the British soldiers. General Henry Proctor, commander of the British forces from Detroit, had even visited her home during this time. Conflict ignited over the Empire's interference in American trade and also over the support Britain granted to Indians in the frontier. (Ohio was still considered the frontier in 1812.)

During the War of 1812, Elizabeth helped the Americans win a decisive battle. The Battle of Fort Stephenson was instrumental in turning back the British. For three days prior to the battle, British soldiers and Indian warriors occupied the area. Elizabeth and her family were in the fort. She asked the commander of Fort Stephenson, Major George Croghan, for permission to approach the British lines to seek information about her son-in-law. He allowed her to go. Elizabeth Whitaker used her close ties to the Indians to find out the plans of Tecumseh and General Henry Proctor. Drawing on her knowledge of British habits, sign code, and multiple Indian dialects, she found out when, how, and where the attack would be launched. She reported her findings to Croghan, who used the information to formulate his defense.

The British granted permission for the family of Nancy Wilson, wife of British Captain William Wilson, to leave the fort before attacking. Though Nancy was deceased, the British were familiar with Elizabeth, her other children, and her grandchildren. Elizabeth and their family left the fort to head for General Harrison's depot at Upper Sandusky. However, Elizabeth remembered she left some important papers in the fort. Her daughter, Rachel, quickly returned to the fort to recover the papers. Rachel could hear the cannons in the distance as she left the area, the last woman to leave Fort Stephenson before the attack.

The battle took place on August 1 and August 2, 1813. Fort Stephenson's defenses totaled one cannon—a six-pound field cannon known as "Old Betsy." Croghan moved the cannon to different locations along the perimeter wall of the fort to give the impression it was more fortified. One hundred sixty U.S. soldiers and a single cannon turned back an invasion force of over two thousand British and Indians—a staggering defeat.

This plaque on the site of Fort Stephenson tells the story of Major Croghan's successful defense.

After their defeat at Fort Stephenson, the British and American Indians realized who was to blame. In an act of retaliation, the British burned down the Whitakers' store, warehouse, house, crops, and orchard—the first and only orchard in northern Ohio at the time. They also slaughtered her livestock and stole a silver tea service—a thank you gift the British had given her years before. Elizabeth had buried the tea set, but they found it. British gunboats on the Sandusky River fired on the area known as Whitaker Reserve.

Before the battle, Britain held the Detroit and Lake Erie region. The British failure to take Fort Stephenson compelled them to retreat. They faced further losses in the Battle of Lake Erie and subsequent battles. The battle of Fort Stephenson was the final western battle fought in U.S. territory. Major George Croghan, the twenty-one-year-old commander of Fort Stephenson, earned a promotion to Lieutenant Colonel for his victory over the British forces.

The Whitaker family was safe, but their home and their livelihood were destroyed. The United States commissioners, General Cass, Duncan, McArthur, and General Harrison, appraised the amount at $8,000. They promised damages would be paid by the government, since it was lost giving aid to the government forces. Elizabeth's family was left with little. Her own assets, banked in Detroit and Montreal, were denied her, as the British who controlled those areas now considered her an enemy. She appealed to General Harrison: "My necessities life, — the ennimy came and plundered and burnt our buildings – and your arms has taken my corn and hogs that the ennimy left. I hope your Honour will consider the distressed the fatherless and the widow in the prayer of your humble petitioner. Elizabeth Whitaker."

During the War of 1812, most of the Wyandots under Tarhe, the Crane, were friendly with the Americans, though some fought alongside the British and Tecumseh. The Treaty of 1817 used this fact to justify again placing the American Indians on reservations. The Wyandots were given land near what is Upper Sandusky in Wyandot County. Other tribes were given land in parts of what is now Seneca and Sandusky County.

Elizabeth acted as a liaison between the Wyandot tribe and the United States government during treaty negotiations. A letter written to Lewis Cass, Governor of Michigan Territory, dated July 6th, 1817, states, "Mrs Whitaker wishes to inform you that the Chiefs of the Wyandot Nation at Upper Sandusky on the 20th of June and left them on the 28th during which time she was devoted to the purpose of consulting the chiefs respecting the intended treaty." Cass responded on July 12, 1817, and wrote "You deserve great credit for your exertions on behalf of the United States, and in the framing on the treaty your services will not be forgotten."

The Treaty of Fort Meigs was signed September 29, 1817. Below is a portion of the Treaty of Fort Meigs, including the reference to Elizabeth Whitaker.

September 29, 1817

Articles of a treaty made and concluded, at the foot of the Rapids of the Miami of Lake Erie, between Lewis Cass and Duncan McArthur, commissioners of the United States, with full power and authority to hold conferences, and conclude and sign a treaty with all or any of the tribes or nations of Indians within the boundaries of the state of Ohio, of and concerning all matters interesting to the United States and the said nations of Indians on the one part; and the sachems, chiefs, and warriors, of the Wyandot, Seneca, Delaware, Shawanese, Potawatomees, Ottawas, and Chippeway, tribes of Indians.

Article 8. At the special request of the said Indians, the United States agree to grant, by patent, in fee simple, to the persons hereinafter mentioned, all of whom are connected with the said Indians, by blood or adoption, the tracts of land herein described:

To Elizabeth Whitaker, who was taken prisoner by the Wyandots, and has ever since lived among them, twelve hundred and eighty acres of land, on the west side of the Sandusky river, below Croghansville, to be laid off in a square form, as nearly as the meanders of the said river will admit, and to run an equal distance above and below the house in which the said Elizabeth Whitaker now lives.

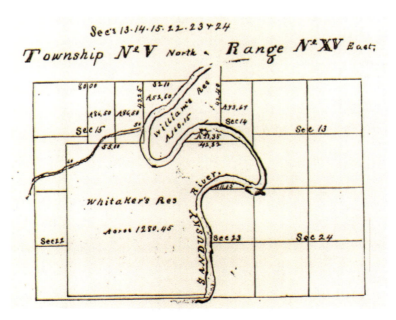

Map of Whitaker Reserve.

> **Township 5 North. Range 15 East 1st Mer. Ohio**
>
> South | Chs | Lks | Between Secs 14 & 15
> --- | --- | --- | ---
> | 30 | 00 | Muskalunge Creek 50 lks wide Course E.
> | 43 | 25 | Intersect N. boundary of Whittaker Reservation at the N. cor of same, on Bank of Sandusky River. [No post or bearing trees noted]
>
> East | Chs | Lks | Between Secs 11 & 14
> --- | --- | --- | ---
> | 32 | 10 | To left Bank of Sandusky River. Set post fr which a Hickory 18 ins diam bears West 275 lks dist. Land 2nd rate, Timber Oak, Hickory &c.
>
> **Survey of Whitakers Reserve**
>
> Courses | Chs | Lks | Began at the Widow Whitakers house; thence
> --- | --- | --- | ---
> East | 1 | 50 | to a Stake on left bank of Sandusky River thence up stream
> S 13 E | 10 | 00 |
> S 19 E | 13 | 00 |
> S 9 E | 12 | 00 |
> S 2 E | 10 | 00 |
> S 7 E | 10 | 00 | Set a post. Return to Stake first set on the Bank of River; thence
> N 7 E | 7 | 00 | Thorn bottom land.
> N 29 E | 9 | 00 |
> N 53 E | 11 | 50 |

In 1822, Elizabeth received a government deed for the lands. However, she could not transfer them without permission from the President of the United States. In 1823, President Monroe allowed her to sell the land to her son, George, for $1,200.

Elizabeth continued to try to get the $8,000 due her from the United States government. Her attorney, Solomon Sibley, was now a member of Congress, and the United States

Attorney for the Michigan Territory. A letter she wrote to him in 1823, requesting help, follows. (Another letter written to Sibley is in the appendix.)

Lower Sandusky, January 5, 1823

Honored Sir:

I wish you to bring my business forward at the present session of Congress and I hope you will succeed in getting my claim allowed by the Government.

I have written to Govenor Cass and the Honorable Sloan, the latter gentleman I have referred to you for any information or explanation he may want concerning my claim. Those gentlemen, I hope will give you their influence and assistance.

I feel satisfied, you will do everything in your power to have my claims allowed. I shall be happy to hear from you.

I am very respectfully Sir
Your obedient servant

Elizabeth Whitaker

During this time, the area Elizabeth lived in experienced rapid growth into an important economic center. In 1821, Lower Sandusky became the county seat of Sandusky County. The community fished and built ships. Farming was also important. It had several saw and flour mills and boasted the first sugar mill in Ohio.

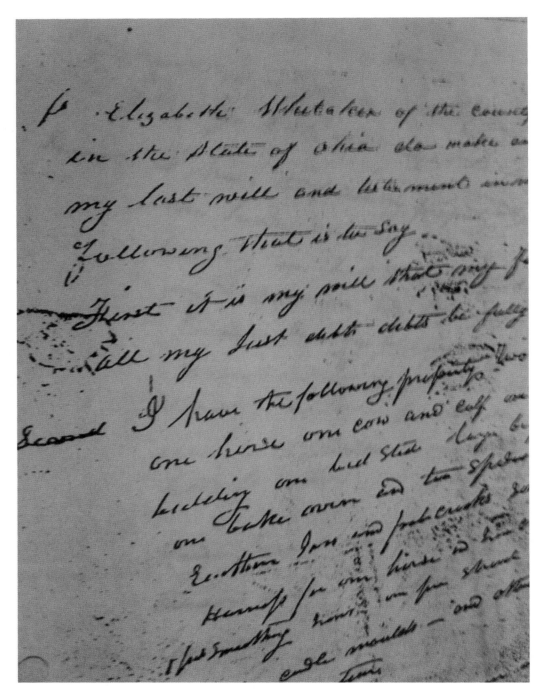

Reproduction of Elizabeth's last will and testament.

Chapter 8
That brave and stout-hearted woman

Elizabeth made several trips home to Beaver Creek, PA. The first was when her eldest, Nancy, was nine months old. Her last trip home was in 1823 for a family reunion. She visited the home of a sister who had twenty-four children (two had died). The sister had a set of quadruplets—all boys—who received green cloth as a gift from President Monroe. At the reunion, the boys were dressed in suits made from the cloth.

During her trips home, she brought back seeds and cuttings to improve the food supply. She introduced the white navy bean. She brought cuttings of the currant bush and apple seedlings. She had the first apple orchard in western Ohio (which the British burned in 1813). She taught the Wyandots to keep bees in hives and harvest their honey.

Elizabeth bore twelve children by James. Four did not survive infancy or childhood. Five daughters and three sons lived to adulthood. Elizabeth survived four of her daughters. Her sons moved to other states.

Elizabeth died in 1833 in Upper Sandusky. Her will was written by her on February 15, 1833, and probated September 13, 1833; her grave is unmarked. There is no confirmation where her remains are. They may still be in Upper Sandusky.

SANDUSKY O. WILL OF ELIZABETH FOULKES WHITAKER- 1833

I Elizabeth Whitaker of the county of Sandusky in the State of Ohio do make and publish this my last will and testament in manner and form following, that is to say

First it is my will that my funeral expenses and all my just debts be fully paid.

Second I have the following property: two mares and two colts, one horse, one cow and calf, one steer, 1 sheep, two beds and bedding, one bedstead, large brass kettle, 3 iron pots, one bake oven and two spiders, 2 cruets, 6 earthen jars and crocks, some crockery, 2 new tin buckets, harness for one horse and his chains, one side saddle, bridle 1 pr. smoothing irons, 2 spinning wheels, a clock, candle molds and other small articles of household furniture.

I also have claims proven on the U.States to eight thousand dollars and ... for spoilation during the last war.

I also have a judgment against Hugh Pattinson of Sandwich U. Canada, Richard Pattinson Surity, about thirteen hundred dollars rec'd 1811, I believe.

I have also claims on my brothers George and William for my share of my father's estate.

I have also a chest containing valuable articles now in the possession of Harvey J. Harrison.

I give and bequeath the above property to my sons Isaac, George and James Whitaker: my daughter Rachael Scranton, and Eliza Wilson and Ann Wilson heirs of my daughter Nancy. The children of my daughter Mary to them one share to be equally divided share and share alike my children.

The children of Mary Shannon to be charged six hundred dollars advanced to her in her lifetime. Also my son Isaac to be charged one hundred and eighty six dollars for two horses, a saddle and bridle, property that Isaac took and carried off.

It is also my will that of the share which shall be coming to Isaac, the interest only shall be paid to him annually during his for life; and at his death shall be paid to his children, my executor investing the amount in some productive fund. I do hereby appoint my son James Whitaker my executor of this last will and testament, in case that my son James should not survive me, I humbly appoint Harvey J. Harrison.

In witness whereof I have hereunto set my hand and seal the 15th day of Feb. 1833.

Elizabeth X Whitaker

Signed checked and sealed in the presence of Giles Thompson and Rebecca Thompson

Here is an inventory of her personal property at the time of her death:

Chest containing articles of silver, including:

Silver caster and cruets	$21.00
8 tablespoons	$16.00
6 teaspoons	$3.00
1 pair of sugar tongs	$1.00

Other items:

1 horse	$35.00
1 mare	$35.00
1 year old colt	$16.00
1 cow and calf	$12.00
1 year old steer	$5.00
1 sheep	$1.50
1 sow and 4 pigs	$3.00
1 dandy wagon	$10.00
1 side saddle	$6.00
1 1-horse stage	$1.50
2 feather beds and pillows	$18.00
1 mackinac blanket	$1.75
1 coffee mill	$.87
2 coverlets	$6.00
22 pieces of calico (47.5 yards)	$9.50

Elizabeth's will mentioned $1,300 that Hugh Pattinson still owed her, as well as the $8,000 due from the US government.

Several heirs tried in vain, to claim the money promised by the US government after the British attack on the Whitaker Reserve. Elizabeth's granddaughter, Ellen Scranton, even made a trip to Washington, D.C. to request the $8,000 in reparations. Affidavits of settlers were presented. The family also sent the papers to Congressman Frank H. Hurd, who represented the area. But no money was ever seen.

On August 2, 1906, the *Fremont News* published a transcript of a letter written by Isaac Ward, who's grandfather worked for Elizabeth. He calls Elizabeth "that brave and stout-hearted woman." And goes on to say, "By reason of her having contributed material and valuable aid to Major Croghan in the defense of Fort Stephenson, which services rendered Croghan and his brave little band of heroes, not only intimately associates Grandmother Whitaker's name with Croghan's victory, but so closely was she identified with that military event which hinged upon the victory gained on that day, that her name was a household word in the homes of the settlers of northwestern Ohio."

James Allen Scranton, 1824–1913. Son of Rachel Whitaker, grandson of James and Elizabeth Whitaker.

Chapter 9

A barrel of rotten pork

Among Indian tribes of the time, the Wyandots were particularly accepting of the white ways and ideas. They adopted the use of log cabins and wool blankets. They appreciated the new crop methods of the white man, as they produced better harvests. They were the final American Indians to leave Ohio, in 1842, when they traded their land for land further west—what is now Wyandotte County, Kansas. In 1867, they were relocated to the northeastern part of the new Indian Territory, now part of Oklahoma.

The Whitakers are considered Ohio's First Family. Their log cabin was built along the Sandusky River in 1782. Marietta was not founded until 1788.

There are several descendants of the Whitakers who still live in the Sandusky County, Ohio area, including Shannons and Scrantons. The first Shannon, and Scranton, in the area, each married a daughter of James and Elizabeth Whitaker. There are many stories about these descendants as well.

George Shannon was born in New York in 1787. He moved to Lower Sandusky in 1809, where he met and married Mary Whitaker. George and Mary had eight children together. Two of their sons, James and John, stayed in the area and had families. After the War of 1812 was over, the family lived in a cabin on a piece of land given to him by Elizabeth Whitaker. One day he was out working the fields when an Indian yell startled the family. Mary called to her husband, but he did not hear her. He was attacked by an Indian with a tomahawk. George gained control of the tomahawk and was ready to kill the Indian when the Indian shouted "friendship." George ordered the Indian inside demanding to know why he targeted him. The Indian asked if he was Joe Williams. "No, my name is Shannon," George replied. The Indian said he had been told Joe Williams lived there, and Joe had sold him a barrel of rotten pork.

Rachel Whitaker married James A. Scranton on April 21, 1823. James died in 1851 while Sergeant-at-Arms of the Ohio State Senate. Rachel died in 1862. They had ten children, three of whom survived to adulthood: James A. Scranton, Ellen Scranton, and Hannah (Scranton) Stoner. Ellen never married. Hannah owned a dressmaking shop in Fremont. Arthur Scranton, Rachel's great grandson, recalled hearing stories his grandfather told of his great-grandfather's travels between Columbus and Lower Sandusky.

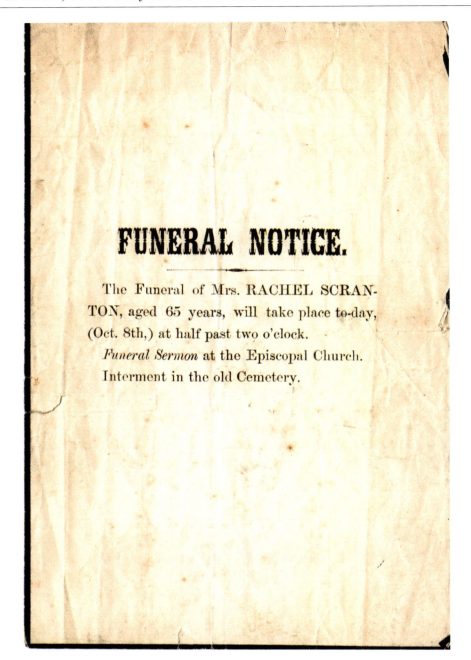

Funeral notice of Rachel Scranton.

Ellen died on Monday, December 17, 1906, in Fremont. She had given an interview to the local paper, *Fremont Daily News*, in August 1905 about her grandparents. She shared many stories from her mother, Rachel. According to her obituary, the family had still had not received money owed them from the United States government for the retribution attack on Whitaker Reserve by the British in 1813.

James Allen Scranton, grandson of Rachel Whitaker Scranton, died January 29, 1913, at age eighty-nine. He had four children who survived into adulthood: Perry Scranton, Will Scranton (who moved to Vestaburg, MI), Emma Scranton (who married James Ulch), and Henry Scranton. James Allen was buried in Oakwood cemetery in Fremont. His wife, Jane

Philo Scranton, died at age ninety-one on September 9, 1921. Perry Scranton died December 19, 1930.

Sardis Birchard built a home called Spiegel Grove, near the tree where Peggy Fleming was tied. His nephew, Rutherford B. Hayes, moved into the home in 1873. Three years later, Hayes was elected the 19th President of the United States. He loved telling his guests the story of Peggy Fleming. Her tree remained on the property until it was too rotten. It was removed in July 2008. The remains are now in the Hayes Presidential Center, which is located next to the home. Both are on Spiegel Grove land. A small plaque on a rock remains where the tree once stood. The first presidential library in the United States is the Rutherford B. Hayes Presidential Center, founded 1916 in Fremont, Ohio.

This boulder marks the original location of the tree Peggy Fleming was tied to when she was held captive in Spiegel Grove. The tree's remains were moved indoors upon its death to protect it from the elements.

Elizabeth was the first white woman to have raised a white family in what is now Ohio. She was brave and courageous. Despite her loyalty to the Indians, she proved to be a good American as well by helping defeat both the British and Indian tribes at Fort Stephenson.

Appendix:

1.) Date issues.
2.) Letters concerning Elizabeth Whitaker.
3.) Descendant information, census data.
4.) Daniel Boone.
5.) American Indian words.
6.) Time line.
7.) Additional pictures.

Date issues.

An interview with Ellen Scranton, Elizabeth Whitaker's granddaughter, in 1906 states that Elizabeth was captured in 1776 when she was sixteen and met and married James five years later, in 1781. She also provided info about James' birth year, 1756, and that he arrived in New York at age twelve.

Homer Everett, a historian of Sandusky County, interviewed Rachel Whitaker sometime after 1815. Everett's book said James was captured in 1774. Rachel gave the most details about the gauntlet run and capture, including that Quill, James' brother, was at Fort Pitt with him. She also stated that Elizabeth was eleven when captured.

Col. Webb C. Hayes states that Elizabeth was captured in 1776, when she was eleven. He also has James being born in London in 1756. He has them married in 1782. He wrote that all their children were born at Whitaker Reserve, the 1280 acres given to them by the Wyandots.

In 1868, an interview was done with George Foulks Whitaker, the youngest son of Elizabeth and James, who moved to Hannibal, Missouri. He states that James was captured in 1778 at age eighteen, Elizabeth was captured in 1780 when she was eleven and that his parents married in 1782.

Most of the history written by descendants of George Foulks states the date of Elizabeth's capture as 1780, including articles written by Mina Foulks and Thom Foulks. These are posted on ancestry.com and in the *Daughters of American Revolution Magazine*, March 1967. Mina says that Elizabeth was nine in 1780 and George was eleven. Letters written by Jessie Davidson, George Foulks son-in-law, have different details. Jessie writes that George was born in 1767, and they were captured March 20, 1778.

A history of George Foulks, Elizabeth's brother, was written by David Bricker. Bricker says George and Elizabeth were captured in 1780 and Elizabeth was fifteen and George was eleven. He also states that James was captured in 1780 and he and Elizabeth married in 1782.

The best proof we have is that on January 5, 1778, the signature of James Whitaker appears on a proclamation issued by British lieutenant governor Henry Hamilton. So, he had to be captured prior to 1778. Also, his tombstone says he was forty-eight when he died in 1804.

Important notes:

Most accounts say James was eighteen when captured. Most accounts have Elizabeth captured two years after James. Also that she was eleven when captured. Most accounts have their wedding five years after Elizabeth captured. Also there are letters dated in 1782 that mention the wedding.

Based on all the information, I have decided that

1.) James was captured in 1774 at age eighteen (so born in 1756);

2.) Elizabeth was captured in 1776 at age eleven (so born in 1765);

3.) They were married in 1782.

With regards to spelling differences, most show the spelling as Whitaker. If it was written differently in letters or on the tombstone, I kept it as the original showed.

Sandusky, August 25, 1807
Mr. Solomon Sibley at Detroit

Sir:

On the seventh of May 1803 by Mr. Patterson's order George Hobbs and a Malotto man named Henry Welch came by night and stole or took a yolk of oxen from Mrs. Whitakers and drove them to the upper Sandusky. On Monday the ninth Mrs. Whitaker rode after them and found them oxen at or near Mr. Pattersons house. Mr. Dougundear was present and heard the abuse. Mr . Patterson of Mrs. Whitaker on the occassion she asked the men who took the oxen by whose orders they took them. The Mr. Patterson replyed by Mine, Madam. In the fall of 1803, the month of November, Hugh Patterson with a number of people in his employ came to Mrs. Elizabeth Whitaker and attempted to pull down with his own hands her hog penn orders his men to assiste in opening the pen and drive away her hogs. In presence of the Wyandott people, the man called Pamp and the Lazy Man, Old Polly and Young Polly and in same year the day before Christmas Mr. Pattirsons people Mr. John Wilson, Old Isaac Williams and Th Williams, a friend came along and shot among Mrs. Whitakers cows and steers and wounded one steer which they killed the thriteenth day after the year 1805. ... and again men in Pattersons imploy came on the 25th December at night after all the family was in bed, attempted to brake her doors and besiege the house.

Wrote by Anne Whitaker for Elizabeth Whitaker and by Mr. Joseph Badger intrepretation.

Sandusky 1821, October 13th
Solomon Sibley Esq
Attorney at Detroit

Sir:

As you are perfectly acquainted with my misfortunes during the last wars , I with more confidence address you and select your friendly advice knowing your ability to give it as will as good wishes for my prosperity.

You will therefore place me under many obligations if you will this once direct me what will be the steps to take to endeavor to obtain some remuninations from government for the many losses which I have suffered. If business of a public nature is not entirely occupying your time I shall be truly thankful if you will be so good as to attend to it for me. Your answer to this with your kind advise instructing me how to act, what papers may be wanted with powers of attorneys forms of certificates, whether or not you would attend my going to the City of Washington will be thankfully

Acknowledging with hears full of gratitude by your obedient servent

Elizabeth Whitaker

Relationship: James Whitaker to James LeRoy Scranton

James LeRoy Scranton is the 3rd great grandson of James Whitaker

Self

James Whitaker
b: 1756
   London, England
d: 17 Dec 1804
   Upper Sandusky, Wyandot, Ohio

Daughter

Rachel Whitaker
b: 1801
   Lower Sandusky
d: 07 Oct 1862
   Fremont, Sandusky, Ohio, USA

Grandson

James Allen Scranton
b: 01 Jan 1824
   Fremont, Sandusky, Ohio, USA
d: 29 Jan 1913
   Fremont, Sandusky, Ohio, USA

Great grandson

James Henry Scranton
b: 1868
   Sandusky Township, Ohio
d: 16 Oct 1948
   Toledo, Lucas, Ohio, USA

2nd great grandson

Arthur Frederick Scranton
b: 17 Mar 1890
   Sandusky Township, Ohio
d: 18 Jul 1973
   Fostoria, Hancock, Ohio, USA

3rd great grandson

James LeRoy Scranton
b: 09 Jul 1946
   Fremont, Sandusky, Ohio, USA
d:

Census information:

1810 Census burned in the War of 1812

1820 Ohio Census data: Sandusky Township, Ohio
Elizabeth Whitaker
1 male 16–25
1 male 45 and up
2 females 10–15
1 female 26–44

1830 Ohio Census data: Sandusky County, Ohio
Elizabeth Whitaker
1 male 20-30
1 female 60-70

Isaac Whitaker
1 male under 5
1 male 10-15
1 male 40-50
1 female 5-10
1 female 30-40

1830 Census: Fremont City, Ohio
James A Scranton
2 males under 5
1 male 40-50
1 female under 5
1 female 5-10
1 female 20-30

1840 Ohio Census: Sandusky County, Ohio—No Whitakers listed.

1850 Ohio Census data: James A., 50, laborer; Rachel, 45; Wm. B, 16, student; Ellen, 13; Hannah E, 10

1880 Ohio Census data: Fremont, Ohio, 2nd ward—Charles Stoner, 40, carpenter; Hannah Stoner, 40, wife; Ellen Scranton, 30, sister-in-law, dressmaker

1880 Ohio Census data: Sandusky County, Ohio—James Scranton, 54, farmer; Jane Scranton, 47, wife; Perry Scranton, 27, son, working in saw mill; William Scranton, 24, son, engineer; Clara Scranton, 21, daughter; Emma Scranton, 19, daughter; Henry Scranton, 12, son; Emit Scranton, 8 months, son

Daniel Boone & Simon Kenton

Two famous captives that came through Lower Sandusky were Daniel Boone and Simon Kenton. They both were taken to Lower Sandusky during their captivity. Simon Kenton was captured in 1778 and ran the gauntlet in the area now known as Piqua, Ohio. The Indian council was going to sentence him to death, but instead sent him to Detroit via a route through Lower Sandusky. Eventually, Kenton moved back to the Ohio area and Kenton, Ohio was named after him. He also served under General Wayne during the Battle of Fallen Timbers. Daniel Boone was captured in 1778 from the Licking River area. The Shawnee warriors took him to Chillicothe then Lower Sandusky and finally to Detroit to meet with Governor Hamilton. Hamilton encouraged Indian actions against settlers and paid a lot for scalps or prisoners. The British would then get a ransom paid by the families of the prisoners. Hamilton liked Boone and offered to buy him from the Shawnee, but they refused. Boone eventually escaped when they took him back to the Chillicothe area.

American Indian words for places in Ohio:
- Auglaize: fallen timbers
- Cuyahoga: crooked
- Erie: cat
- Maumee: muddy river
- Ohio: great or beautiful river
- Sandusky: water within water pools

English:	Wyandot/Wendat words:
One	Skat
Two	Tindee
Three	Shenk
Four	Andauk
Five	Weeish
Longhouse	Ganonchia
Man	Aingahon or Onnonhou
Woman	Utehke or Ontehian
Water	Saundustee

Wendat is the Wyandot's name for themselves, and it means peninsular people. Huron was the French name for the Wyandot tribe. It means "wild boar" in French.

TIME LINE

900-1550	Late Prehistoric Indians known as the Fort Ancient people build settlements in area known as Ohio.
1580s	French explorers and Jesuit missionaries explore area known as Ohio.
1700s	About 20,000 American Indians lived in Ohio area.
1750s	French construct trading post in Lower Sandusky (now Fremont).
1754-1763	French and Indian War (Seven Years' War) between Great Britain and France. American Indians support the French.
1756	James Whitaker born in England.
1763	France loses Seven Years' War. Treaty of Paris signed. Ohio area is under British control.
Dec 25, 1765	Elizabeth Foulks born in Leesburg, Virginia.
1767	James Whitaker arrives in New York.
1768	Treaty of Fort Stanwix signed.
1774	Foulks family moved to area now known as Beaver Creek, Pennsylvania.
1774	James Whitaker captured near Fort Pitt, PA.
1775-1783	American Revolutionary War takes place. Most American Indians support the British.
March 20, 1776	Elizabeth Foulks captured near Beaver Creek, PA.
August 1782	James and Elizabeth Whitaker marry.
1783	Nancy Whitaker born.
1784	Isaac Whitaker born.
1787	Northwest Ordinance passed by Congress. Ohio is part of Northwest Territory.
1788	Marietta, Ohio founded.
March 20, 1790	Peggy Fleming captured.
1791	Mary Whitaker born.

April 29, 1791	Daniel Convers captured.
Nov 4, 1791	Battle of St. Clair.
March 1, 1793	Nathan Goodale captured.
August 20, 1794	Battle of Fallen Timbers.
August 3, 1795	Treaty of Greenville signed.
1801	Rachel Whitaker born.
March 1, 1803	Ohio becomes 17th state.
1803	George Whitaker born.
Dec 17, 1804	James Whitaker dies.
1804	Nancy Whitaker Wilson dies.
1812	War of 1812 begins.
August 2, 1813	Battle of Fort Stephenson.
September 10, 1813	Battle of Lake Erie.
1816	Columbus becomes Ohio's capital.
1817	Toledo, Ohio founded.
Sept 29, 1817	Treaty of Fort Meigs signed.
1821	Lower Sandusky is made county seat of Sandusky County.
1833	Elizabeth Whitaker dies.
1843	Wyandots, Ohio's last tribe, leave Ohio for reservations in the west.
1876	Rutherford B. Hayes elected 19th President.

Additional Pictures

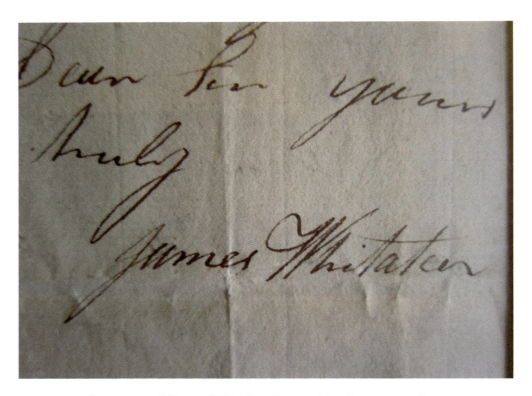

Signature of James Whitaker from original correspondence

Signature of Elizabeth Whitaker from original correspondence.

From L-R: Emma Scranton, James Henry Scranton, Nina Scranton Lewis, Daisy Scranton, William Scranton. William and James Henry are the sons of James Allen and Jane Philo Scranton.

From L-R: Emma, James Henry, and their son, Arthur F. Scranton, ca. 1905, in front of their house on County Road 234.

From L-R: Back row: Perry Scranton, Meta Scranton, James Henry Scranton, Ralph Parks, Arthur Scranton, Mrs. Parks, William Scranton, Emma Scranton Ulsh, George W. Scranton, Edna Scranton, Claude Welliver. Front row: Don Welliver, unknown female, Evelyn Welliver, unknown but possibly Emma Peters Scranton, Jimmy Parks, George Scranton Jr., Laverne Scranton, Daisy Scranton. Photograph dates from the 1920s.

The letters used to tell Elizabeth and James' story can be found, along with many more original letters, at The Burton Historical Collection at the Detroit Public Library, Detroit, Michigan.

Road sign for the Hayes Presidential Center at Spiegel Grove.

Ohio historical marker for Spiegel Grove.

Detail from the plaque marking the location of the tree Peggy Fleming was tied to when James Whitaker and Chief Tarhe rescued her from the Cherokees.

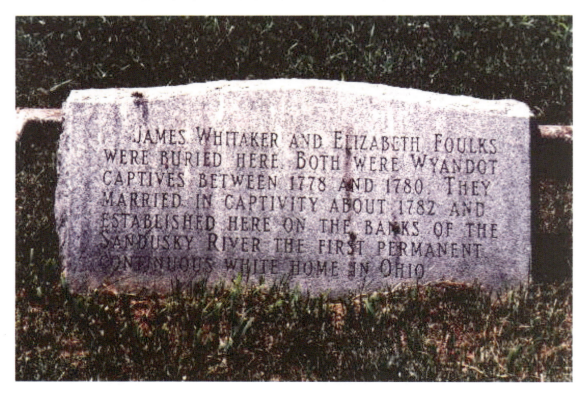

Grave marker of James and Elizabeth Whitaker.

WORKS REFERENCED

"Brave Elizabeth Whittaker" *Fremont News* August 2, 1906.

Bricker, David D. The George Foulkes Story Updated. Milestones Vol 25 No 4 http://www.bchistory.org/beavercounty/beavercountytopical/ColonialandEarlysettler.html

Burton Collection, Detroit Library. Hull papers. Sibley papers.

Danner, John. *Old Landmarks of Canton and Stark County, Ohio.* Logansport, Indiana: B. F. Bowen publisher, 1904.

Doherty, Craig A. and Katherine M. Doherty. *The Huron.* Vero Beach, FL: 1994.

Draper Collection—Wisconsin.

Everett, Homer. *History of Sandusky County, Ohio.* Fremont, 1882.

Foulks, Mina. "Elizabeth Foulks Whitaker" <u>Daughters of the American Revolution Magazine</u>. March 1967.

Foulks, Thom. http://www.foulks.com/family/thefoulks.html

Hayes, Webb C. *James Whitaker Family.* Fremont: n.p., n.d.

Keeler, Lucy. *A Guide to the Local History of Fremont, Ohio Prior to 1860.* Columbus, 1905.

Ohio Census of 1820.

Ohio Census of 1830.

Ohio Census of 1850. "James A. Scranton Residence." 16July1850.

Ohio Census of 1880.

Peninsular Farms History. http://www.sandusky-countyscrapbook.net/peninsular/history.htm

"Perry Scranton Pioneer is Dead." *Fremont Daily News.* 25Dec.1930, C5.

"Pioneer Woman is Called Home." *Fremont Daily News.* 10Sept.1921, C3.

United States. National Archives, Records of Michigan Superintendency of Indian Affairs. "Letters Received and Sent." Vol. 2.

United States. National Archives, Records of Michigan Superintendency of Indian Affairs. "Lewis Cass letterbook, outgoing correspondence." Vol. 4.

"Was Early Settler." *Fremont Daily News.* 30Jan.1913, C2.

"Reminiscences of George F. Whitaker, son of Elizabeth Foulks" *Wisconsin Historical Collections.* Frontier Retreat, pp. 152-153.

<u>Whitaker Ancestry Booklet</u>. N.p.: n.p., n.d.

Workers of the Writer's Program of the Work Projects Administration in the state of Ohio.

Fremont and Sandusky County. Columbus: Ohio State Archaeological and Historical Society, 1940.

Wyandot Indian Fact Sheet. http://www.bigorrin.org/wyandot_kids.htm

**Unless otherwise noted,
all photographs and illustrations
are from the Scranton family collection.**

Made in the USA
Lexington, KY
08 October 2016